ALL ABOARD!

MONORAILS

Phillip Ryan

PowerKiDS
press.

New York

Published in 2011 by The Rosen Publishing Group, Inc.
29 East 21st Street, New York, NY 10010

First Edition

Editor: Joanne Randolph
Book Design: Ashley Burrell
Photo Researcher: Jessica Gerweck

Photo Credits: Cover Richard Cummins/Getty Images; p. 5 © www.iStockphoto.com/James Bossert; p. 6–7 Shutterstock.com; p. 9 © Jim Corwin/age fotostock; p. 10–11 Jorg Greuel/ Getty Images; p. 13 © Dennis MacDonald/age fotostock; p. 14–15 Getty Images; p. 17 © Walter Bibikow/age fotostock; p. 18–19 © Jeff Greenberg/age fotostock; p. 21 Jenna Bodnar/Getty Images; p. 22–23 Shutterstock.com.

Library of Congress Cataloging-in-Publication Data
Ryan, Phillip.
  Monorails / Phillip Ryan. — 1st ed.
     p. cm. — (All aboard!)
  Includes bibliographical references and index.
  ISBN 978-1-4488-0638-6 (library binding) — ISBN 978-1-4488-1217-2 (pbk) — ISBN 978-1-4488-1218-9 (6-pack)
  1. Monorail railroads—Juvenile literature. I. Title.
  TF694.R936 2011
  625.1'03—dc22
                                    2009048770

Manufactured in the United States of America

PSIA Compliance Information: Batch #WS10PK: For Further Information contact Rosen Publishing, New York, New York at 1-800-237-9932

CONTENTS

Do you know what a monorail is? This is a monorail waiting at a **station**.

Monorails are trains that ride on one **track**. Can you see the track here?

Monorail trains look different from other trains. They have parts that go around the sides of the track.

Monorail tracks are often high up on **beams**. They run above streets and parks.

Sometimes there is room for only one train on the beam.

Some beams have two tracks. Trains going different ways can then use the same beam.

14

Some monorail trains do not ride on top of a track. This one in Tennessee hangs from its beam!

Monorails take people where they need to go.

Monorails are made up of parts called **cars**. People sit inside the cars.

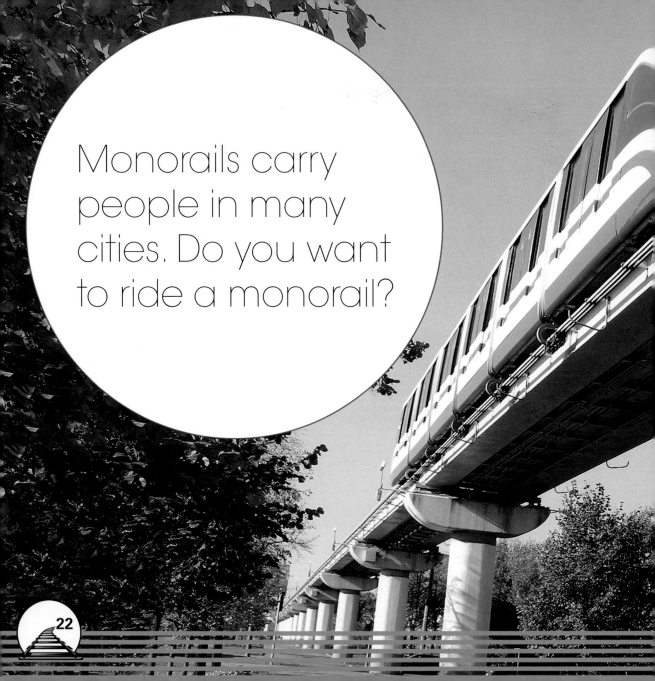

Monorails carry people in many cities. Do you want to ride a monorail?

WORDS TO KNOW

beam

cars

station

track

INDEX

WEB SITES

Due to the changing nature of Interr
links, PowerKids Press has develope
an online list of Web sites related to
subject of this book. This site is upd
regularly. Please use this link to acc
the list:
www.powerkidslinks.com/allabrd/m